# THE NEW HOME
# COLOR BOOK

ROCKPORT

# THE NEW HOME
# COLOR BOOK

Decorate With Color Like a Professional Designer

ROCKPORT

PUBLISHERS

Anna Kasabian

First published in the United States of
America by
Rockport Publishers, Inc.
33 Commercial Street
Gloucester, Massachusetts  01930-5089
Telephone: (978) 282-9590
Facsimile: (978) 283-2742
www.rockpub.com

ISBN 1-56496-809-X
10 9 8 7 6 5 4 3 2 1

Design: Francesco Jost
Cover Image: ©Eulenburg/Picture Press

Printed in China.

# CONTENTS

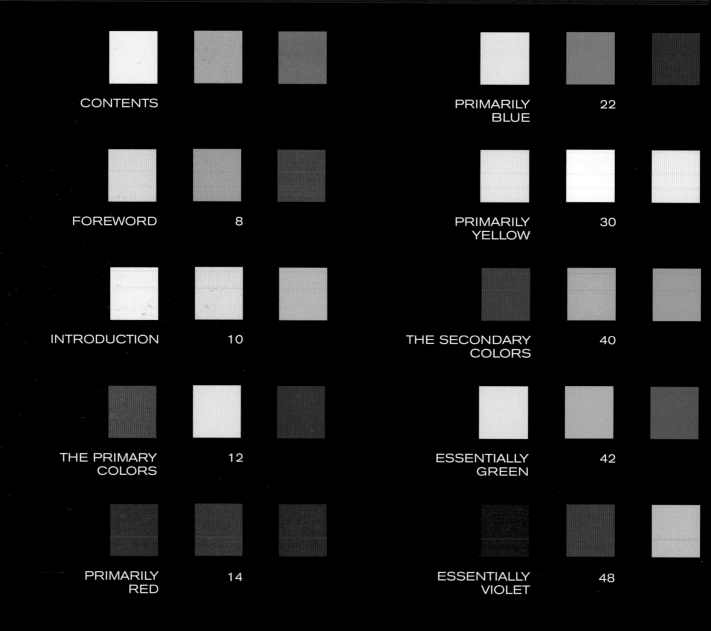

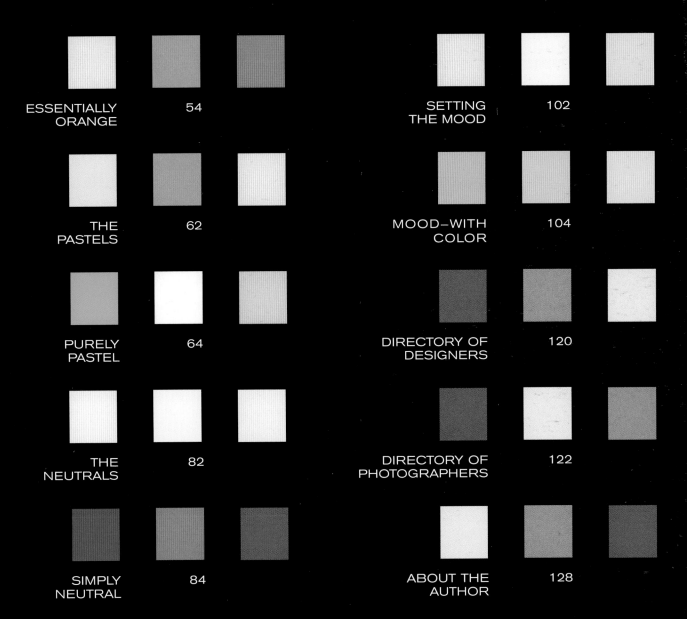

# foreword

In researching the topic of color I spoke with more than 40 experts, and most agree that too many people choose colors that don't really reflect who they are. As a result, their individual spirit and energy never surface in their homes. The purpose of this book is to help you think a bit outside the box on color, encourage you to experiment, and through tips and examples, find your true palette.

We kept text to a minimum in order to give you a quick read with informative, sometimes amusing, nuggets from top experts, a virtual Who's Who of the design world, to help you think new color thoughts. I had the pleasure of interviewing some of New York's finest, among them interior designers Mario Buatta, Jeffrey Bilhuber, Alexandra Stoddard, and Thomas Jayne. Equally enjoyable were my interviews with President Clinton's and Senator Hillary Rodham Clinton's person-al White House designer, Kaki Hockersmith; HGTV's Joe Ruggerio; author, designer, and television host, Chris Madden; and Alexander Julian, who has his own line of home design products.

As you turn these pages, looking at the all the rooms, make note of which colors please you. Then once you've gone through the entire book, review where you might begin to experiment with a new palette. It could be as small a step as wallpapering a guest bedroom, or painting the inside of your pantry drawers red! Think too of the words of author and art expert Halima Taha: "The experience of color is about how color informs us, inspires us, and titillates the senses." Make this your color mantra, and go!

# introduction

Too many of us feel like deer in headlights when it comes to choosing a color theme for our rooms. And, too often, we stick with the safe choices in paint or wall coverings to avoid taking a big design leap.

I am convinced part of that fear of making a color faux pas comes from a lack of inspiration. Studying paint chips in a fluorescent—lit store is enough to set anyone into permanent color daze!

So in the spirit of inspirations in color, *The New Home Color Book* presents an immense array of rooms divided into color—denoted chapters to give you a fresh look at ways to use color in your home, and ultimately, motivate you to take a color path you've never ventured down before.

To enjoy, appreciate, and then move on to experimenting with new color palettes takes practice and exposure. Remember the first time you tasted an unusual ethnic dish while traveling? You were perhaps hesitant at first, but the more dishes you tried and the more you came to understand the people, their culture, and their culinary ways, the more excited you became to sample more dishes. And maybe when you came home, you started experimenting in your own kitchen with a new herb or sauce from that trip.

Color is no different. It takes some getting used to, and sometimes it's easier to start with little bites! If you've always had white walls and a white couch with beige pillows, perhaps this book will give you the confidence to toss the beige pillows for a medley of red, orange, and yellow ones.

Get ready to be drenched in the color experience, and listen as the experts cheer you on to take a new color leap.

—Anna Kasabian

the primary colors

the new home color book

# primarily red

Sometimes just accenting a room with red is enough to change the spirit. The bright red couch and multicolored curtains with big blocks of red combine nicely to pull this cheery room together.

Some people like red but tend to shy away from it in their décor because it's a big color and makes what they feel is too strong a statement. If you'd like to use red, but don't want to overwhelm your space with it, consider introducing it in a way that will bring out the qualities you admire. Take a step back and think about how you can take the color and gently weave it into your roomscapes.

## The Red Range
The great thing about red is that its range is very dramatic, which gives you many opportunities to use it in different rooms and create distinctly different moods. Deep, dark, rusty red can create the perfect warmth for a library or establish an elegant mood in a dining room. On the other end of the red spectrum, the palest of pinks combined with moss green and yellow can be the perfect backdrop for an ultra-feminine dressing room. Introduce tomato red with bright yellow accents to a kitchen, and even on the dreariest winter day, you'll feel energized.

## Bringing Red Into the Scene
Think about the level of red you want to introduce in your home. It can come in many forms, and you can easily turn the volume of red up or down. Here are a few of the ways to bring on the red:

• Upholstery: For a splash of red, one red velvet chair; for more, an entire red couch. Choose a pattern with other colors, and work off that as your palette.

• Wall coverings: As an accent, choose one red for one wall and create a scene that shows off an elegant table and glass vase. For a bigger statement, paint an entire room fire engine red and weave in deep, dark blues and crisp whites with furnishings.

• Window treatments: Drama comes through loud and clear if you paint your walls linen white and frame your windows in an apple red. Accessorize with rugs that blend rich red tones with warm hues or cool, depending on the mood you want.

• Art: Use red to subtly jazz up a low–key décor with art–whether it's a glass collection in shades of red or paintings with red as the main color.

• Floor covering: Work with red only in your rugs, and build a palette from the ground up. The warmth and drama can build up and around the room.

## Red Combinations
On the color wheel, red moves from rich, spicy hues all the way to pale, dreamy pink tones. Consider these combinations:
• Red and green
• Three consecutive hues or tints of red
• Red and blue
• Red in a variety of tints

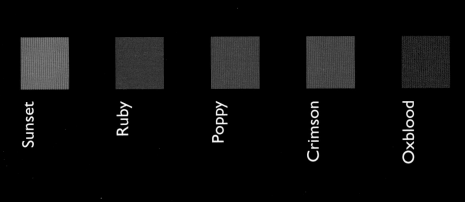

Sunset   Ruby   Poppy   Crimson   Oxblood

Don't want to paint your walls red? How about the ceiling? This windowless corridor glows in a cocoon of ruby-red and gold and leads the way to a light-filled room in a similar palette. Notice how the lamps, little red box, and art splashed with red combine to complete a look.

**When red takes the lead, it makes a statement about you and how you like to live. This elegant living room shows how red to the max can pull together a fresh, dramatic look, all the while holding onto a bit of tradition.**

**The bright red walls in this bedroom provide an interesting backdrop for the art, and the white draperies maintain the peace that belongs here.**

**SUSAN MOORE,
A MINNESOTA-BASED COLORIST:**

"Everyone thinks the wall with art should be white. I have 56 pieces of art with color behind it. I think when you have, for example, a painting with a lot of red in it and you put it against a green wall, it becomes important; you create a focal point.... I find a lot of people who like red [and] use it as the color they don't have in their lives; they use it to motivate themselves. They're usually introverts! I told some-one who said they wanted more courage to do something that they should buy some red underwear! Red is about bravery and courage."

**NEW YORK– AND BOSTON-BASED INTERIOR DESIGNER CELESTE COOPER:**

"In one project, the client specifically asked for red. And here I used it on lacquered walls in the dining room, picked it up as an accent on seating in the kitchen, [and added it in] a leather insert in the floor, handrails in the foyer, and on little tables in the living room. In this case, the most important issues were balance and repetition."

**NEW YORK–BASED INTERIOR DESIGNER
LEE BOGART:**

"I use red a lot, a real tomato red. It's a wonderful color choice when you don't have a lot of architectural detail. When you walk into a red room it makes a wonderful statement. To me it's a neutral because you can use it with brown, blue, pink, and yellow tones."

**CHRIS CASSON MADDEN, A NEW YORK–BASED DESIGN EXPERT, AUTHOR AND
FURNITURE DESIGNER:**

"I have to admit that 18 years ago I did paint an old pine library red, and took steel wool and glazed over it. It glows in the dark! When people hear I've had a red room in my life they can't believe it...but I needed that secret red room. Now we're loosening up about color, and loving it."

**KAKI HOCKERSMITH, INTERIOR DESIGNER
FOR THE WHITE HOUSE UNDER THE
CLINTON ADMINISTRATION:**

"I think red, one of my favorite colors, is the most challenging to work with.... I might go through four or five paint sample books before I find the right one because there aren't that many good choices."

**Keeping the palette simple in this dining room with bright red walls and soft beige fabric anchors the elegant mood.**

**Choose a monochromatic theme in deep, rich colors to maintain a mood. Here, rusty red walls and matching fabrics give this room a warm glow year round.**

If you want to show off your art, set it on
a deep-colored background. In this eclectic
room, each piece of art and each element
of the various collections stands out—
perhaps just what the owner wanted!

A collection of red pillows in different color combinations provides the perfect dash of color and drama to an all-white room. This color strategy frees you to experiment with color with little financial commitment.

Talk to a paint expert about bringing texture to your walls with different painting techniques. Here, the red-brown walls have been sponge-painted in a swirling pattern that accentuates the rich palette. Notice, too, how the art, frames, rug, and fabrics share earthy tones, and how each stands on its own against the wall of color.

**PARIS-BASED INTERIOR DESIGNER SYLVIE NEGRE:**

"In the North of Paris we have a lot of 'silver days,' so in sophisticated flats I will prefer to use a lot of darkish red. It helps to warm it up. Then, on a wall, you can have yellow or terra cotta, or a large stripe with white, green, and red, or even material from old French fabrics..."

**BARBARA MAYER, NEW YORK–BASED AUTHOR, LECTURER, BENJAMIN MOORE ARCHIVE CONSULTANT:**

"My kitchen is an example of a color scheme I've had for over 20 years. It's Chinese red on the top cabinets, and the inside is painted sunny yellow. Every time I open those cabinets I get a great deal of pleasure. In fact, it was the kitchen cabinets that made me decide to get more color in other rooms."

**JEAN TOWNSEND, PROFESSIONAL PAINTER AND CO-OWNER OF DROLL DESIGN:**

"I always seem to have a red room or [red] furniture in my home—but colors are made more pleasurable by the things that are put next to them. The power of the vocabulary of color rests on the relational aspect because color is a vocabulary, just like language."

Blue walls become exquisite trimmed
with pearl white: subtle accents of black
in picture frames and furnishings suggest
a stylish, French influence.

Blue is one of those ubiquitous colors that, once you look for it, you are bound to find it somewhere in most homes. It could be a tiny dash subtly woven into a patterned rug, or in the bright blue sky of a painting, but it's there somewhere! Like red, in its deepest, darkest tone, blue is a big color, and it makes a statement. But unlike red, it's a statement that is easier to manipulate. Perhaps you've ignored blue—thought it only works with a certain furnishing style, or that it's confining. Let go of those notions! Think of blue as a color that can add depth to your home's palette.

## The Blue Range

The densest version of blue is midnight, and moving a few spaces from that on the color wheel is blue with a bit more red in it. Both are dramatic and as strong in attitude as red. We commonly see these versions of blue in dressier, elegant spaces where dark woods prevail and the mood is well defined by accessories. These hues are literally light years in mood from paler versions like baby blue or the green-blue robin's egg blue. The latter can come into your design scheme in fabrics with a floral motif, where contrast plays hard, or through subdued monotone silks that can set the stage for the sublime. Dark blues give you a backdrop that can enrich a simple room or echo the lushness of a high-in-detail, architect-urally complex room. Move down the light scale and you create space that sings spring or spa.

## Bringing Blue Into the Scene

Following are some ways to bring varying shades of blue into your home palette.

## Light Blues

Blue has a reputation for being soothing, calm, and sometimes cool. Choose the palest blue hue that appeals to you, and bring it into a room where those qualities matter. Using blue in its palest form gives you the latitude to accent it with other colors you normally migrate toward. The blue-green tones are reminiscent of the island environments and spas, and work well in bathroom, sunroom, or bedroom. Pinks, yellows, oranges, and like hues can be added to complement and hold the theme. Choose pale blues with red tones and you work up a richer palette with shades of red or gold. Remember, you don't have to make a big color commitment, such as with gold furnishings or fabric. It can be as simple as accents via art in gold frames.

## Deep Blues

Think cobalt or midnight blue to make a statement and anchor a distinct mood in a space. Imagine your dining room painted with a high-gloss or lacquered midnight blue effect-set against a rich mahogany wainscoting. Keep the ceiling white and you've created an elegant cocoon that will glow with candlelight. If the thought of your living room in either of these shades seems over the top, consider bringing them in if only for the window treatment. Imagine a yellow-on-the-verge-of-gold wall with rich, midnight-blue brocade drapes. Another way to introduce dark blue is through your bedding. Imagine off-white bedroom walls encircling a cobalt blue comforter—pillows piled high with a warm or cool palette with deep blue accents.

## Blue Combinations

Remember the color translates the mood when considering combinations. Play with versions of light and dark, warm and cool to find the look that pleases you most:
• Blue and gold • Blue and yellow
• Blue and red • Blue and orange
• Blue and green

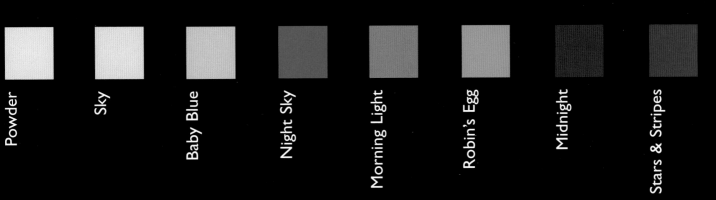

Powder

Sky

Baby Blue

Night Sky

Morning Light

Robin's Egg

Midnight

Stars & Stripes

Kitchens don't always have to be energized and hot. Here a pale blue kitchen with light blond wood makes for a serene workplace.

The contrast of a bright yellow ceiling and equally electric blue wall gives this kitchen area a distinct personality. When you use color like this, "stacked up," so to speak, it provides a unique canvas for decorating. Colorful glassware anchors the crisp white cupboard into the space and enhances the overall view.

Before you paint, think about the views from one room into another. Here a bright-blue dining room looks into a bright-green library—the pleasant change and contrast easily leads the eye from one place to another.

**ALEXANDRA STODDARD,
A NEW YORK—BASED INTERIOR DESIGNER:**

"I like to have blue in my home because of the sky, and water, green because of the land, and yellow because of the sun...all the colors that I love for my work are inspired by nature. In one way or another I try to bring these nature references to where we live because I think we are starved for them!"

**NEW YORK–BASED INTERIOR DESIGNER
ZINA GLAZEBROOK:**

"I've chosen to live near the water so the palette I respond to comes from sand, the colors of beach stones and shells, the ocean's blue grays.... I find blue [to be] elegant."

**PARIS–BASED INTERIOR DESIGNER
ERIC SCHMITT:**

"I generally use raw white for the skin of the house. I also use pure white in isolated places to add light. I like strong color in very bright rooms; I generally use rather dark and strong shades like China red or slate blue."

**JEFFREY BILHUBER,**

**A NEW YORK–BASED INTERIOR DESIGNER:**

"We always do an icy, frosty version of blue in a bedroom. Most people say they want a warm pink or yellow, but those colors work in the complete reverse because you will look blue in rooms that color. If you use blue in the room, it brings out your color as warm skin tones. Test this by holding your hand up to a cool color and see how your skin looks!"

**CHARLES SPADA,**

**A BOSTON–BASED INTERIOR DESIGNER:**

"If I'm talking to a woman client about color, I notice what colors she wears. We're hoping to do this new apartment and the owner wears the most beautiful soft colors. Her favorite is green—blue, and I want to pick that for her [home] because it works with her skin tone and eyes."

**WASHINGTON, D.C.–BASED INTERIOR DESIGNER, MARY DOUGLAS DRYSDALE:**

"I think there's a resurgence in the use of color. Why? Because there is a certain sort of dullness that sets in and people get tired of seeing the same old same old."

Look at how a simple palette with blue as the star works in this sitting room. The crisp, geometric qualities of this black-and-white tile floor provide an unexpected, attractive contrast in tune with a crisp, neat theme.

Periwinkle walls, in combination with bare windows, welcomes the blue of the sky and natural light in this peaceful bedroom. With barely another color in the room, it holds its Zen qualities.

Here is a room that exemplifies the
benefits of bringing just the right blue and
yellow together in a theme. Tossing the
yellow pillows across the sea of a blue
couch is a great touch, and the island of
green and yellow in the foreground adds
yet another element of color interest in
the space. Notice, too, how the neutral
walls make the fabric the star.

Consider giving family photos, dressed in rich gold frames, a solid color anchor of blue.

# primarily yellow

Yellow makes a perfect "neutral": warmer and more sumptuous than white, it works well as a backdrop for dark or black furnishings, and heightens the honey tones in polished wood floors

How can anyone not like yellow? It says so much to us that is positive. We smile when the sun comes out, and when it sinks down into the horizon. And, nearly everyone on the planet photographs yellow's many moods in nature. It is a color of cheer, warmth, and light, for sure, and it's no wonder fabric, wallpaper, and paint manufacturers give us so much to choose from in the yellow range. Used sparingly or not, yellow glows on—rarely creating a negative mood in our space.

## The Yellow Range
Yellow's range moves from green-yellow to bright lemon-yellow, to golden—all the way down to the faintest shades of butter.

As a green-yellow, it is commonly used as an accent color or to saturate an ultra—modern, sculptural furnishing that's making a big design statement. Think of green—yellow as more of a focused hue that's got its color antenna up for what it complements. Some trendy, hot designers have been using this shade in the new, hip hotels and restaurants, and it is making its way into the more confident color lovers' homes.

Brighter, purer yellows that remind us of buttercups or daisies are often a good fit in period rooms, where they set up an engaging visual plane of contrast with deep, dark woods. Rooms seem to glow in these tones and with snowdrift white trims, and ceilings, bright yellow presents a crisp, clean, energized space. These same hues also find their way into kitchens, where the warmth of the hearth, and the rays of morning sun combine to sustain a cheery palette.

With the paler yellow hues, the mood moves from cheer to a calm, steady glow. The more white added, the more distant the yellow, and the more latitude to accent and contrast.

## Bringing Yellow Into the Scene
There are no rules on where yellow works best in a home. In fact, it's one color that really looks as attractive in a bedroom as it does a den. Just remember, the intensity of the color sets the mood.

Imagine how a den that lights up with the late afternoon setting sun will look in a deep, golden yellow. That color will take the natural light and emphasize warmth year round. In summer, you can tone it down by introducing other cooler accent colors via throw pillows or curtains in a new palette.

Take advantage of yellow's intensity by using it in a low—light hallway, entryway, kitchen, or tiny powder room. Accent it with other warm colors like red, orange, or peach to direct the yellow focus. Turn to shades of green and brown as accents and you can create a more earthy, calm, casual mood in a library, study, or sunroom. Whatever you choose, you can blend in snow white, other shades of yellow, and even black to punctuate architectural details.

## Yellow Combinations
Try finding real examples of these to help you visualize how well they work together and spark your imagination:
• Yellow and red
• Yellow and green
• Yellow and purple
• Yellow and orange
• Yellow and blue
• Yellow and pink
• Yellow and lilac

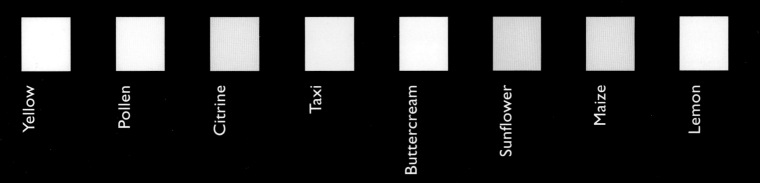

Yellow • Pollen • Citrine • Taxi • Buttercream • Sunflower • Maize • Lemon

What are you looking to create in your room? How do you want to feel? In this bedroom, a nature-themed palette of green and yellow with dark woods is peaceful and warm.

If you use yellow as the main color in your window treatment, you can make a dramatic statement—especially if you have a room with high ceilings like this one. Also, if you are in a north-facing room, the color can help you get through low-light days. Keeping the ceiling white gives the room more light, and using an open floral with complementary colors really ties up a look.

If you choose not to paint a wall yellow, but you would like the effect it brings, look for art to do the job. These panels of yellow not only satisfy the inhabitant's craving for yellow, they set off the soft blues that make up a secondary color theme.

**JEAN TOWNSEND, PROFESSIONAL PAINTER**

"I'm naturally drawn to a high-key color palette in my artwork. But the for the colors I prefer to live with, those would be too bright. I'm most comfortable around old things, weathered, with dings, that have some sign of hav-ing had a life, and when that happens to satur-ated colors, it mellows them a bit. That's when you get old-feeling colors like Sicilian yellow! In order to get colors without bite you have to gray them down, and to do that you add their complement to the paint. So to get yellow to be softer, you put a little purple in the paint."

**KELLY HOPPEN,
LONDON INTERIOR DESIGNER:**

"Yellow is a color I never use if I can help it. I always think it looks tacky, and is very difficult to use as well."

**ANTHONY ANTINE, NEW YORK–BASED
INTERIOR DESIGNER:**

"Yellow is my favorite color. It makes a room always have sunshine, and makes me happy. I like it buttery and creamy, I find other versions too harsh."

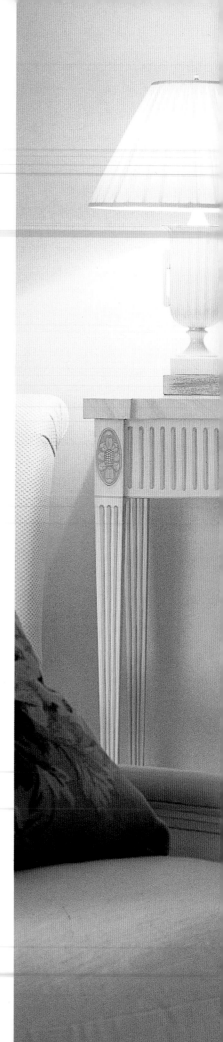

**KAKI HOCKERSMITH, INTERIOR DESIGNER**
**FOR THE WHITE HOUSE UNDER THE**
**CLINTON ADMINISTRATION:**

"The common denominator at the White House is yellow or gold, and that's a happy, sunny color. They [President Clinton and his wife Hillary] really like color, and natural light which is the reason they enjoy bright pastels..."

**EVA DEWITZ,**
**A BOSTON-BASED INTERIOR DESIGNER:**

"I find that lemon yellow is very harsh and in a north-facing room, will actually seem strangely cold. For pale yellow I like the yellow-cream color of rich vanilla ice cream or I use yellow with a hint of orange to retain warmth of the color no matter the compass direction of the room."

**TREENA CROCHET,**
**A BOSTON-BASED INTERIOR DESIGNER:**

"I'm from the South and I painted my entire Boston home in shades of yellow. I need the sunshine, and when I don't get it I get real sluggish. I used four variations of yellow in my home, and now when it's gray outside, I'm energetic!"

**Whenever you take color to its palest form, you give yourself the most freedom to go elegant. Buttery yellow walls provide the perfect frame for soft, curvaceous, furnishings.**

To create a clean, crisp, modern look, consider lemon-yellow walls. This will frame and accentuate furnishings and art.

**ZINA GLAZEBROOK, A NEW YORK–BASED INTERIOR DESIGNER**

"It's wonderful when you have a blank canvas, like a guest room—take a big color leap here. It's not a room you're in all the time... For rooms you are in a lot, it's nice to have them clean, and neutral, especially those filled with everyday objects. It keeps it peaceful."

**ANTHONY ANTINE, A NEW YORK–BASED INTERIOR DESIGNER:**

"If I had a dark hallway with one window I would paint the hallway yellow with a linen white trim and a bright white ceiling. I'd keep the stairs natural or walnut. The darker the floor with light walls, the more height."

**WASHINGTON, D.C.–BASED INTERIOR DESIGNER MARY DOUGLAS DRYSDALE:**

"Everyone underestimates the power of yellow. It's strong. You take the light value of it and all of a sudden this mousy color turns into a lion, so you have to be very careful with the hue you choose."

**What better way to brighten and add cheer to a room than with lemony yellow? Keeping the palette simple by adding only white to the scheme can also be calming.**

# color now

Joe Ruggerio, the host and producer of multiple home design television series and specials aired worldwide on The Home & Garden Television Network (HGTV) says after completing extensive research, he recently identified three new color and home design trends:

1. The Boulevard: This, he says, includes the monotones, the putties, and the black accents. "It's what we saw in the lofts in London and Paris—easy to live with and peaceful. Furnishings were sculptural and unadorned."

2. Spice: Colors are tropical like spice, curry, guava. "We see that coming into the fabric market, and that's for the people into an ethnic, more adventurous, romantic palettes," he says.

3. Euro Country: Here is a palette that reflects the countryside. "It looks collective and ancient. And with new technology, we can take a tapestry fabric and wash and aerate it to make it look puckered and old. This palette is terra cotta, beige, gold, sage, green, and a muted lemon/citrus..."

(Ruggerio has been a multimedia design authority figure to consumers for many years. He is most noted for bringing the subject of home design to network television. He was chief design consultant to the PBS award-winning series, **This Old House**, where he designed and decorated nine houses for the show. He was also a design correspondent on ABC-TV's **Good Morning America**.

the secondary colors

# essentially green

The most beautiful greens mimic nature.

If green were a person, it would probably be a world-renowned peacemaker. Gentle on the eye, whether it's deep, dark forest green, or the palest lime, green is a color most of us can introduce without creating a color war within our walls. In fact it works well with nearly every color on the color wheel, and can, by its honesty and range, be worked into schemes that excite, calm, comfort, and embrace us.

## The Green Range

Some shades of green have more blue in them, and these tend to be cooler, richer, and perhaps more suitable to a formal mood. The moss greens, which have more yellow in them, are warmer, and therefore offer more possibilities for a variety of rooms and furniture styles. As you move down into the lighter hues, the pale greens with a hint of blue, for example, and the moss that evolves to pale lime, the door opens for many who may initially shy away from green as a wall color. At its palest point, green can easily be envisioned by most anyone as complementing upholstery or window treatments where various shades of green mingle with rich or not-so-rich colors. It becomes a soft background that can echo a theme, quietly.

## Bringing Green Into the Scene

Green gives you the base to create or support many themes. Here are a few ideas:

• Go country: A home with a casual atmosphere might come into its own with grass or apple greens, the tones with more yellow in them. A country-style kitchen works well with either shade on the walls, the cabinets, or the floor. Painting the floor in a high-gloss green, or covering it with stone or tile with a green tint, keeps the nature theme and frees you to accent with other warm, countryside colors like red or orange. A warm, terra-cotta color floor would also work well here.

• Make a bathroom feel like a spa: The most soothing form of green is the lightest, and whether you choose a blue-green or pale lime, either will hold the calm you desire. Accent with deeper, richer towels if you like, or complementary pale colors such as sand, chocolate brown, pale yellow, peach, blue, or white.

• Bring the outside in: Whether you live in Hawaii or Paris, bringing the outside in via an all-natural palette makes a space pleasing, relaxing, and easy on the eye. Consider giving green the lead in a sunroom, living room, or study—especially if these rooms have outdoor views. That way, the palettes can dovetail, and further support the visual illusion! Use dark, blue-greens to richen the room and enhance the coziness, or lighter hues with complex, multicolored prints that recall spring.

## Green Combinations

Remember, you can also have all of these together if you want—it's just a matter of balance. You may find a fabric, for example, that incorporates all these colors, and launch the décor from there with appropriate wall color and window treatment choices.
• Green and red
• Green and yellow
• Green and blue
• Green and orange

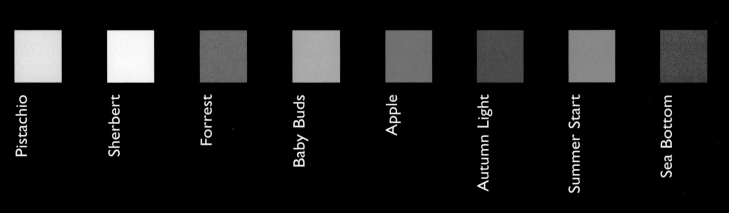

Pistachio    Sherbert    Forrest    Baby Buds    Apple    Autumn Light    Summer Start    Sea Bottom

If you truly love green, this room shows you how to make it work with different fabrics, tones, and complements.

Yellow and dark green provide a pleasing combination in this country-style kitchen, and keeping the light color on the walls works especially well with the natural light. The dark green background works well to show off the yellow dishes and knickknacks.

Here is a study in the beauty of simplicity. A dark wood floor provides the pedestal, if you will, for soft, sculpted furnishings. Borrow this theme for a bedroom, bath, or dining room.

**KELLY HOPPEN,**
**A LONDON-BASED INTERIOR DESIGNER:**

"As for green, I used to use a lot of this with black, the dark racing green, and celadon as an accent."

**LAURA BOHN,**
**A NEW YORK–BASED INTERIOR DESIGNER:**

"My favorite color is green, green, and green —all shades except forest, ivy, or kelly; lime is okay. Green is the most soothing, and I see it as a neutral because I can put any kind of wood or color on top of it. It really looks great if you mix it with blue and yellow. And, it totally relates to nature."

**MINNESOTA-BASED ARCHITECT**
**KATHERINE HILLBRAND:**

"I love greens and purples. I think of green in certain ways though. I'm not an emerald-green person. I like dusty greens, and I think that has to do with being in the woods and the shadows. I'm drawn to an emotional love of trees, so it's primeval. And I do believe in genetic memory, and believe my history had something to do with the forest."

**ALEXANDRA STODDARD,**

**A NEW YORK-BASED INTERIOR DESIGNER:**

"It would be hard for me to think of a room without having green in it. Interior environments are supposed to echo nature. And blue is the most prevalent in our universe because of the sky! Often, I paint ceilings blue, walls pale green with white trim, or pale yellow walls with white trim. And if I wanted to echo the sunset, I would paint the walls pale pink, and the ceiling pale green."

**BOSTON-BASED INTERIOR DESIGNER**

**CHARLES SPADA:**

"I think if you want a really beautiful green, go walk through a dappled forest in June and look at the moss in the sunlight, and the shade. There's a palette [beyond] compare! I think its crazy to depend on paint companies to come up with color schemes; you should come up with your own colors."

**NIK RANDALL, AN ARCHITECT WITH BROOKS**

**STACEY RANDALL, LONDON:**

"I do not think of colors so much in terms of preferring yellows to greens for example, but rather about how a color or series of colors can work with a space to enhance the architecture."

The strategy here was to bring the outside in—or merge the views, green on green. You can do the same with wall paint, wallpaper, or tile, building on texture and variety many ways.

Notice how these pale, mint-green walls allow the architectural details of this minimalist-styled room to shine through. This would work in any room where you want peace and color quiet.

# essentially violet

Experiment with dynamic color combinations in places where they'll be appreciated. Here, a child's bedroom embraces city life, illustrated in bold hues of purple, lilac, blue, and gold.

It seems people either take to violet from the start, and use it confidently, or they just don't ever warm up to it. One reason might be because it is not commonly used, so none of us has a lot of exposure to it. Often, violet enters design schemes quietly as supplements to fabric patterns or as a punctuation point in rooms—big, satiny pillows strung across a contemporary couch, as regal, flowing velvet drapes, or as a single purple chair that makes a statement. If you're on the fence about violet, consider this chapter as a place to get a new view. Perhaps you will be inspired to try it in a room that needs a color boost and a dash of drama.

## The Violet Range

In its darkest form, violet is dramatic, moody, and a natural for rooms where formality reigns—deep purple, burgundy, and eggplant, for example. And depending on what colors and patterns it's combined with, it can turn distinctly playful, feminine, or masculine. As white is added, and it becomes more enriched with light, it takes on a less formal mood.

## Bringing Violet Into the Scene

If you're venturing into the world of violet for the first time, intrigued at its potential to define a mood or to just break up a monotonous palette, tread lightly. For example, if you have a sleek, contemporary couch in either white, brown, black, or gold, add violet in richly patterned or solid dark brown pillows, or throws. Or, take that tiny powder room and paint it the darkest violet you can find. Accent it with a collection of gold-framed mirrors to create a regal room, or silver-framed pictures to support a clean contemporary theme. You might also try choosing a wallpaper pattern in which violet takes the lead in that powder room, and

accent the paper with purple towels and rugs. This way, you won't be making a huge violet commitment, but you'll have freshened your palette and upped your interest level. If, on the other hand, you're ready to take a bigger violet step, consider using it in a room you can accessorize with colors you do normally relate to and can integrate easily—perhaps in your bedroom, dining room, or in its deepest shade, a study or den. Pastels work nicely in the bedroom—pale violet, pink, yellow, and green, for example. In more public rooms, deeper shades might be the best choice.

## Violet Combinations

When you combine violet with other colors, you can create an interesting and unusual palette because it is a color with a high surprise factor, and that alone can make it fun to work with. Some combinations to consider follow. And remember, from dark to light versions, these combinations are distinct and compelling:
• violet and gold
• violet and lime
• violet and tomato red
• violet and gray
• violet and apple green and gold

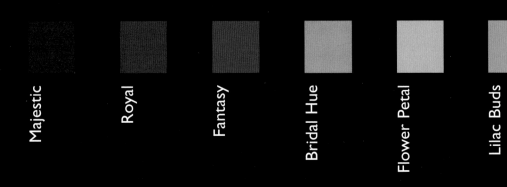

Majestic    Royal    Fantasy    Bridal Hue    Flower Petal    Lilac Buds    Pansy

Lilac walls and a little purple chair accent give this sitting room a unique flavor. Use a combination like this on a smaller scale just as successfully. Try lilac walls in your dressing room or bath, and accent with wallpaper that has a purple theme. Accessorize with burgundy, deep purple, and lilac with a floral scatter rug, towels, and glass soapdish or vase.

**Purple, blue, and lilac take what could have been a small, boring, square dining area, and transform it into a striking space where color reigns.**

**MICHELLE LAMB, A COLOR TREND WATCHER BASED IN MINNESOTA:**

"No one has ever asked me my favorite color!... I am pleased to tell you it's purple, and it's been that since the twelfth grade. In the past I have liked it against stark white; today I like it with pinks, greens, and particularly against a green-cast yellow called natural cane. I also like purple that is influenced by brown. In my color forecast I call it plum—brown, and it's an awfully exotic color."

**NORTH CAROLINA ARCHITECT SARAH SUSANKA:**

"I've gone through phases. I had the phase of rust reds and reddish tones, then greens. Now I'm now in my purple phase, and mauves, with a little red rust. And I'm wearing purple too! I recently bought a dark blue couch and chairs, and it goes well with my rug that has blue, green, mauve, and purples in it."

**THOMAS JAYNE, A NEW YORK—BASED INTERIOR DESIGNER:**

"I think purple is hard to use, and it may be because of the religious overtones, or because it looks like bad satin lingerie."

**NEW YORK INTERIOR DESIGNER**
**JAMES RIXNER:**

"Lilac always reminds me of spring and a re-freshing renewal of the spirit. I use this color when I'm conveying a youthful, fresh feeling. It has a positive energy that plays well with many other colors."

**CHRIS CASSON MADDEN, DESIGN EXPERT,**
**AUTHOR, FURNITURE DESIGNER:**

"Lavender is the new color, and if you want to be au courant, [toss] a lavender throw into a room or a plumb leather chair or chaise, or pillows. I don't think home design is about trend[s] but a lot of people like to spark up a room, and bring in the color for the season."

**MARY DOUGLAS DRYSDALE,**
**A WASHINGTON, D.C.–BASED**
**INTERIOR DESIGNER:**

"Get some foam core and experiment with paint. Discover what you like. Pick a color family and play. See what you respond to, and then ask yourself 'what is this color do-ing for me. Does it make me feel like I'm in the country, sophisticated, etc.?' Then go a step beyond and create your own palette."

**Most people would be hard-pressed to imagine a purple living room, but as demonstrated here, going monochromatic can work quite well, producing a soft, peaceful place.**

Pale violet walls framed in white is
an unexpected combination for a dining
room, but it works quite well to create
a pleasant space. Introducing rose and
lilac at the table support the spring-
like palette.

# essentially orange

**Combine orange and pure white to create a space that is peaceful and bright.**

Orange is easy to integrate into a color scheme because it is compatible with so many colors. Just a touch of orange in a room can dramatically alter the spirit and energy level. As you move through this chapter, think about how you might adapt one or more orange hues into your home palette. It can, by its dramatic tonal range, be a very useful decorating tool.

## The Orange Range

Think of a summer sunset and you will be reminded of orange's beautiful range—from the deepest red-orange down to the softest, palest yellow-orange. At its darkest tone, orange is energized and emits warmth; at its lightest, when it moves from salmon to peach, it's as peaceful as dawn. Orange works in any room of the home and can be used with both dark and light furnishings, contemporary or traditional.

## Bringing Orange Into the Scene

There are many ways you can introduce orange into your décor, be it just an accent to another color, or as the dominant color in your design palette. Here are a few ideas:

• Introduce orange at eye level under kitchen cabinets to brighten the work area.

• Paint the inside of a windowless walk-in pantry a shade of burnt orange and accent with yellow.

• Use a cheery shade of yellow-orange as the backdrop for your sun porch or sunroom, and add accents of green and gold. Mix in a floral print via pillows or seating Consider orange taking the lead in a young girl's or boy's bedroom or bathroom. Accent with deep shades of blue and green or pink and yellow.

• Take the richest hue of orange and brighten up the stairway to your basement—save yellow or bright blue for the banister!

• Pull swatches of the palest shade of orange and pair it with an equally pale blue-green for a spa-like bathroom, dressing room, or peaceful, feminine study.

• Find a fabric you love that integrates shades of orange and use it as a bed canopy, window treatment, or to recover your favorite reading chair and footstool. Consider painting one wall of that room in a solid shade of dark orange and the other three in a very pale shade.

## Orange Combinations

Remember, orange is versatile and highly compatible. Try using three or more of these colors in fabrics, floor treatments, artwork, or other decorative elements.
• Orange and yellow
• Orange and green
• Orange and blue
• Orange and purple
• Orange and black
• Orange and pink
• Orange and red

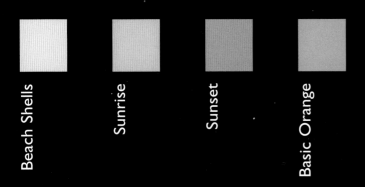

Beach Shells    Sunrise    Sunset    Basic Orange

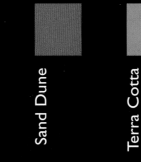

Summer Sun    Sand Dune    Terra Cotta

Gold and burnt-orange give these spaces a pleasant color base for furnishings and art. Introducing earthy tones like brown, gold, and moss green in couch pillows and accessories maintains a peaceful mood.

**CELESTE COOPER, A NEW YORK–
AND BOSTON-BASED INTERIOR DESIGNER:**

"I think color is a very personal thing. For instance, I hate orange but it certainly works for Hermes! I have never refused to work with a client's favorite color but I might, for instance, try to use that orange as an accent and not on the walls!"

**KELLY HOPPEN,
A LONDON-BASED INTERIOR DESIGNER:**

"Orange, if it is burnt, is an amazing color, and works well with neutrals."

**MARY DOUGLAS DRYSDALE,
A WASHINGTON, D.C.–BASED INTERIOR
DESIGNER:**

"I love warm colors. The palette I feel comfortable with is pumpkin to yellow. I love them because they're vigorous and optimistic. There's the relationship to the sun and warmth. On a sunny day we think we'll conquer the world and if we come into a space and the color energizes, it reinforces optimism."

**When you want a color to take the palette lead you don't have to cover all the walls with it. Just one wall will do, as you see in this bedroom with an Asian flair.**

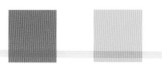

**NEW YORK–BASED ARCHITECT**
**R. SCOTT BROMLEY:**

"I love orange—it's the color of love!"

**ARCHITECT HEATHER FAULDING:**
**NEW YORK**

"Color is and should be the story of everything."

**ALEXANDRA STODDARD,**
**A NEW YORK–BASED INTERIOR DESIGNER:**

"One of the things I feel strongly about is a
lot of people who are afraid of color find these
glamorous names for ugly colors. For example
they call them cinnamon, and the color really
could be called sick puppy poop! Put that all
over a wall and I think it will smell bad!"

**NORTH CAROLINA–BASED ARCHITECT**
**SARAH SUSANKA:**

"The neat thing about paint is you can
change it. I encourage people to get a piece
of sheetrock or plywood if they're painting
outside, and use the color they're contemplating on a large enough piece (near
other things) to better evaluate it."

Orange is as appropriate for a formal
living room as it is for a child's playroom.
In this space, billowy tangerine curtains
move like wet brushstrokes of color
down the lemony walls, creating
an enticing retreat.

Here again, orange take the lead, this time in a living room. The dark color against the all-white furnishings creates a crisp, neat space that's also peaceful.

# color now

Color palettes change with the times, and when they do they affect the colors of the cars we drive, clothes we wear, and homes we live in.

Michelle Lamb, the senior editor of *The Trend Curve Newsletter* is constantly tracking how trends move, and how they affect our homes. Here is what she is observing:

• Warm reds are cooling down; soon we will see more of a blue influence. (That is because orange has become a color family all its own.)

• We are going to use more color in the years ahead and we will use many colors from the same family with different values.

• For color extensions we'll go to an adjacent color family—like pinks moving to purples.

• There will be more palettes that go from pale to deep, allowing us to use complex colors in a simplified way.

• I am hearing something new from people. They're saying I am decorating with this color because it makes me feel this way... This thought has been in our minds but we didn't talk about it! Recognition of that has made decorating more intentional.

the pastels

The palest of blue accented by green bamboo trompe l'oeil provides the perfect backdrop for furnishings in this foyer. Think about how you can use wallpaper to introduce new colors and images in your home.

Pastels, the palest, sometimes translucent versions of color, add dimension to a room without being overbearing, and do not necessarily require a decorating commitment that aligns with the color.

Basically, pastels give the color shy a low-risk opportunity to introduce a number of colors in their home, and in doing so, subtly alter the atmosphere and mood, and define rooms, architectural detail, and art.

Beyond that, pastels, like primary and secondary colors, can be used to anchor a theme. You can, for example, create your fantasy feminine bedroom and dressing room with soft floral wallpaper—a mix of soft greens, peach, and buttery yellow. If you paint the woodwork a complementary color, the palest version of peach, for example, you will further enhance the theme. The palette will blend and form one overall visual. If you chose a dark color, like bright lemon yellow, you would separate the visuals and make a very different statement.

Pastels also work well as a backdrop and complement for furnishings and art, and in the right room, can enhance the play of natural light. If you have a framed floral print on the wall—a mix of pink, purple, and yellow, for example—and you paint the wall the palest form of yellow, you'll draw your eye to the painting's pretty palette. And, if the room is one where afternoon or morning sun is plentiful, that yellow wall will further emphasize the garden theme in your art.

A simple experiment you can conduct without much fuss or expense is to order large paint chips in colors that interest you and hold them next to places you're contemplating their use. That's a tip from Barbara Mayer, author, lecturer, teacher, and historical consultant to Benjamin Moore & Co. She suggests if you're particularly anxious about moving from white walls to color, choose a few shades that interest you, and paint little samples on the wall of the room. Live with it for a week in all kinds of light, and then make a decision.

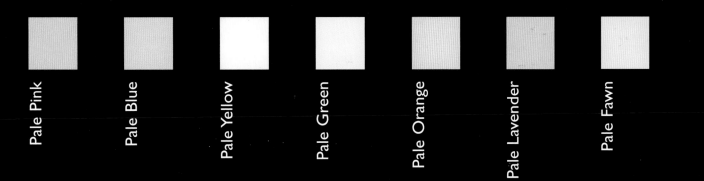

Pale Pink   Pale Blue   Pale Yellow   Pale Green   Pale Orange   Pale Lavender   Pale Fawn

Notice how this barely-there, butter-cast bedroom is the ultimate in serene. The pale, sheer green draperies add just enough color to frame the window without disturbing the peace.

**BOSTON-BASED INTERIOR DESIGNER WILLIAM HODGKINS:**

"I love pastels, and I'm pretty unbiased—except I don't like rusty orange. I love pale pink and soft, soft colors... sometimes they spark things up in a gentle way. I just finished a white room in Palm Beach and made the ceiling pale, pale blue, and the dining room ceiling is the palest aquamarine green... But you need to be careful so things don't look too delicate!"

**RHODE ISLAND–BASED ARCHITECT DAVID ANDREOZZI:**

"Is there anything more paradoxical than pastel colors? Subtle yet distinct, soft yet poignant, soothing yet controlling. These [colors] are dangerous territory because on the face of it they appear very user friendly, yet, the risk is that individual pastel colors seem to go in and out of favor quite often."

**CHARLES SPADA, A BOSTON-BASED INTERIOR DESIGNER:**

"I love pastels, and am growing more and more fond of their subtlety. You can use four or five colors in the softest, palest tones and the result is just wonderful. I go to Greece a lot and on the beaches there are these smooth, round stones, and that palette is so beautiful; I use it a lot. If you wet them, you get even better colors!"

**LONDON-BASED INTERIOR DESIGNER**

**KELLY HOPPEN:**

"I only use pastels as accents. They work with taupe, which is my color, and salmon-pink mauve—but only a small amount, and never as a wall color."

**EVA DEWITZ, AN INTERIOR DESIGNER**

**BASED IN BOSTON:**

"Pastels work best in rooms most often used in daylight, while dark jewel tones reflect artificial light well, thus they shine in the evenings. Pastels will change colors as the day passes and the light outside changes. If you choose pastels for your surroundings do it because you love subtlety and serenity—not because you are afraid of trying the emerald green walls you have always wanted... If the rest of your family can't see living with emerald green walls, paint the inside of your closet that color and smile every time you open it."

**LINDSAY BOUTROS-GHALI, A BOSTON AND**

**SAN FRANCISCO—BASED ARCHITECT:**

"When you say a word that has to do with color, people envision something different from the next person. The images that come to my mind with pastels are Liberty cottons, elegant, sleek celadon, or delicate lemon. I can be really excited by pastels—they're like being inside of a sherbet desert. You can take them into a room and make it serene, bright, and lively."

**If you've ever wondered what a raspberry room would look like, here it is. You either love what it does or not! In this room it contrasts sharply with the traditional furnishings, blending eras and feelings.**

This kitchen uses pastels to the max! Robin's egg blue cabinetry sets off the imaginative backsplash, created with multicolored pottery and dishes. The powder-pink painted cupboard complements perfectly. Soft yellow exude's a mellow glow. If this palette inspires you, but you're color shy, consider toning it down with white and experiment with paler versions.

 Luscious shades of green fabric play off the artwork in this crisp, sculpted room. Here is the perfect example of how less is more.

If you like pink, don't underestimate its potential to take over a room and make a unique statement. Here, the art and rich pink couch are the focal points, while the pink walls and ceilings hold it all together.

In this space, the pale-yellow wall color defines the details of the furnishings, from lamps to sofas to the tabletop. It could easily be reversed, or the palette could be adopted in a bedroom, for example, where the carpet was white and the fabric yellow.

**THOMAS JAYNE,
A NEW YORK–BASED INTERIOR DESIGNER:**

"I think pastels are really valuable, and underrated because sometimes they appear to be very saccharin. But they have tremendous appeal when they are introduced as a color and not a pastel. One of my favorite colors is pink. If, instead of painting a room white you paint it a pale pink or green, [the room] takes on a new life. A lot of modern architecture uses white to show off the volumes of architecture, but I think that is a disservice because I think there is more beauty and volume if you had color. The other thing you can do is make a project hang together by warmth and coolness. Sometimes I'll pick a warm pink and a warm blue for a room (instead of yellow) and it makes it seem more light and brilliant. In my home I use pink, blue, and green. I like them because they're buoyant and they remind me of southern climates."

**CLAIRE MURRAY, DESIGNER OF RUGS,
WALL COVERINGS, HOME ACCESSORIES
AND CLOTHING:**

"I try to be loyal to myself and what makes me comfortable. I absolutely draw from nature. For years my palette has been a range of blues, lavenders, pinks, and greens; I must have a dozen greens in this palette. I love yellows too—they're very comforting and uplifting. I'm not too much for earth colors..."

**JEAN TOWNSEND, PROFESSIONAL PAINTER**

"If you put pink next to white, you're not going to have anywhere near as pink a feeling than if you put pink near frosty green where you'll really feel the pink."

**BOSTON-BASED INTERIOR DESIGNER KAREN SUGARMAN:**

"My husband calls me the princess of pink! I guess I use it a lot. I don't know why I am attracted to it... I've found though that people like to use colors they look good in, and it's a good color for me... Because I am from the South I gravitate less to the muddy colors; I like sunshine and a clearer pastel palette."

**CHRIS MADDEN, DESIGN EXPERT, TV HOST, AND FURNISHINGS DESIGNER:**

"If I did not have my pale peach/parchment bedroom, I would die! I just keep having it repainted the same color over and over. When it's been an insane day, I want to dive bomb into that room. I'll have this color bedroom the rest of my life..."

**Mother Nature's palette is alive and well in this peaceful sleeping space. The lime-green, cream, and brown window treatments and coverlet give the illusion of sleeping deep in the forest.**

**A bright yellow window treatment against pale, seashell-pink walls makes for a cozy yet cheerful space.**

Pale yellow walls are a strong complement to the exposed-beam ceiling in this
country kitchen. The all-white cabinetry
and shelving keeps the space looking
clean and efficient while the dark green
countertops add contrast.

Blue and lilac may never have occurred to you as the right color combination for a kitchen, but a cool, calm palette such as this may help you hold it together in stressful kitchen moments.

A touch of green and little punctuation points of gold and green via fabric frame and accentuate the white furnishings in this elegant living room.

Lime green and dollops of copper and brown in this simply furnished bedroom establish a feeling of Zen.

**LAURA BOHN,**

**A NEW YORK–BASED INTERIOR DESIGNER:**

"Dark colors are good for foyers and dining rooms because at night, with candles, it looks beautiful. I love light-colored kitchens—taupes, greens, white. For baths, I like them to look fresh with pale blues, aqua, clean feeling and spa—like. I love yellow and blue towels with that."

**LONDON ARCHITECT**
**ARTHUR COLLIN:**

"I believe there is no such thing as a bad color. It is context that makes a particular color inappropriate. I use everything (not all at once!) and I prefer a distinctive and challenging use of color to a safe option."

**LONDON ARCHITECT NIK RANDALL:**

"...color should be considered as the design develops and not merely be applied as an afterthought. Too often color is used in an attempt to make a poor design or space seem more interesting. In time, the color will irritate as the space itself is not interesting or does not function."

**LAURA BOHN,**

**A NEW YORK–BASED INTERIOR DESIGNER:**

"Most people's inclination [is] to go bright, but when they get the color home, it's usually much brighter than they thought. What I've told people is to pick your favorite color and take it to the lightest hue to try it."

**LONDON ARCHITECT**

**NIK RANDALL:**

"One should have no preconception as to which color to use. When using color I think it is limiting to start with a preference for, say pastels, or yellows, or greens. One should consider what is appropriate for the situation. I don't believe in favorite colors. Nature uses them all for specific purposes, and that is what makes our environment so interesting. I do not have a favorite color."

**ALEXANDRA STODDARD,**

**A NEW YORK–BASED INTERIOR DESIGNER:**

"To inspire yourself about using color, look at a garden or sky, or field."

**The softest medley of pastels makes this sitting room feel quiet and soothing, and the pale green window frame simply addresses the greenery outside.**

**Here is the ultimate relaxed palette—a pale sky-blue ceiling and buttery yellow walls. What could be better to create just the right mood for sleep. The tree-themed bedcover and complementary patterned rug makes one feel like your tiptoeing through the woods at dawn.**

Nearly monochromatic, this combination of soft lilacs creates a very peaceful living room. Again, you can adopt this for any room you wish and get the same effect.

A warm pumpkin wall absorbs the morning light and creates a cheerful, warm bedroom. Billowing white sheers and a fluffy white down comforter infuse the room with grace.

**BARBARA MAYER, AUTHOR, LECTURER, AND CONSULTANT TO ARCHIVES OF BENJAMIN MOORE:**

"I did have a color experience recently. I decided after many years with all-white walls to paint walls in different rooms different colors, one wall in each room. All of the colors I chose were warm. I'm very glad I did this; white is safe, but it's neat to take a chance with color. I find my artwork that's hung against a colored wall is much more powerful, and gives the artwork more distinction."

**LAURA BOHN, A NEW YORK–BASED INTERIOR DESIGNER:**

"I love anything pale, soft, and soothing. In my loft I have seventeen colors and you never notice them!"

**Mellow yellow could be the title for this gracious bedroom. The chocolate-brown pillars stand like tall trees shading the sun-filled room, and provide attractive anchors of texture.**

**NEW YORK—BASED INTERIOR DESIGNER ZINA GLAZEBROOK:**

"I've chosen to live near the water so the palette I respond to comes from sand, the colors of beach stones and shells, the ocean's blue grays.... I find blue [to be] elegant."

**PARIS-BASED INTERIOR DESIGNER ERIC SCHMITT:**

"I generally use raw white for the skin of the house. I also use pure white in isolated places to add light. I like strong color in very bright rooms; I generally use rather dark and strong shades like China red or slate blue."

Pistachio-green walls and white trim crisp up this little sitting room. Notice how well this works as the introduction to the next view—a lemony yellow bedroom. Think about room-to-room views when deciding what colors you want to use.

the neutrals

Use white and brown to complement art objects that share a view. You wouldn't notice the lines on the vase, or the exquisite muscles on the cougar, if color backed these objects. Also, having the brown precede the white in these rooms provides the perfect visual frame for what's to come.

Neutrals are a major part of Mother Earth's base palette and are therefore both familiar and comforting. Think about the neutral tones we see everyday—sand and soil, variegated soft tones on seashells and stone. In bringing these colors into our homes, we can complement the tones and textures of natural fibers, wood hues, and shapes. In addition, neutrals frame and extend your outside views like no color can.

The all-white or champagne-colored room (walls and furnishings) lets the shape of the furnishings, whether they are ultra-sleek or down-filled and cushy, shine through. The same holds true for a black marble sculpture, or a simple wrought-iron umbrella stand set against a neutral wall. You are not caught up in seeing how color plays off them; rather you embrace the art of the piece.

But, as many designers say, choosing colors is quite personal—it's your point of view and what makes you happy that matters.

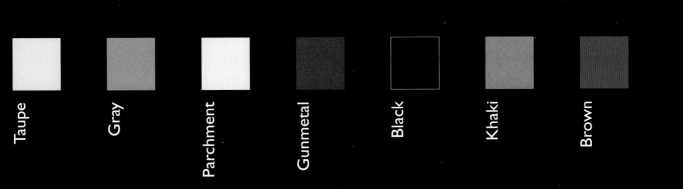

Taupe  Gray  Parchment  Gunmetal  Black  Khaki  Brown

There is something totally serene about an all-white room. You notice the details and shapes you might have overlooked in a room doused in color. In addition, everything has equal importance in the view. When color comes in via a little plant, bowl of apples, or glass, it becomes more art than reality. If you have the slightest curiosity about what you could create with white, but feel a big room is too daring, try it out in an entryway or small guest bedroom.

### KELLY HOPPEN,
### A LONDON-BASED INTERIOR DESIGNER:

"I have spent many hours mixing colors because I could never find the perfect paint. The first collection that I brought out was called 'The Perfect Neutrals'... I discovered that it was not only my belief and passion that neutrals work best as a backdrop for our environ-ments. If you use them as a base, anything you put with it works and one never really tires of it."

### MINNESOTA-BASED COLORIST,
### SUSAN MOORE:

"I like combinations of color; it's all about what they do to each other. My living room is palomino pony (a sand color) and saddle on the ceiling and the woodwork is dark. My dining room is deep red with a saffron ceiling so color bounces all over. And my kitchen is a greenish yellow with a gold ceiling. Everywhere you look you see color!"

### JOE RUGGERIO, HOST AND PRODUCER
### OF HGTV'S *HOME DESIGN* SERIES:

"I like all color. But if I had to pick, I'd look toward my office. It's a sandy, non-color, something you can accent."

**RHODE ISLAND—BASED ARCHITECT**

**DAVID ANDREOZZI:**

"The use of neutrals in architecture, to me, relates a structure to Mother Earth...a red cedar-shingled New England barn, a white cedar-shingled Nantucket boathouse, and a Georgetown brick home have one thing in common...their individual vernacular relationship to their surroundings. To the end ...neutrals provide the base this connection."

**LONDON ARCHITECT**

**ARTHUR COLLIN:**

"All-white interiors are a contemporary cliché. In practice there is no such thing as a standard white and any particular white is not necessarily the same as any other white. Our project for a 'white apartment' in London (shown in London Rooms) embraces the subtle differences that plague color matching by adopting a color scheme using three very subtly different whites. The differences between these whites achieves a subtle decorative effect that results in a warmth quite different to clichéd white minimalism."

There is a lot to see and study in this elegant room—beautiful, rich fabric on the couch and chair, sculpture, and paintings. Using a toned-down palette for all of these things, including the wall, makes for a visually rich, engaging space.

Greenish-gray, beige, brown, and honey
make up the palette of this Zen-like living room and dining area. Keeping the
neutrals as the anchor lets the interesting dark and lightwoods stand out like
free-floating sculptures.

In this big open family living space, the decision to use pale pastel paint and neutral furnishings and carpets works well by allowing the eye to fully appreciate the beautiful craftsmanship of the woodwork, architecture, and in the case of the living room, take in the outside views.

Gunmetal-gray might not be the first color to come to mind for a bedroom, but it works to create a cozy space with a sense of neutrality that is calming and peaceful.

**JEFFREY BILHUBER,**

**AN INTERIOR DESIGNER IN NEW YORK:**

"Obsidian! It's the color of a match strike, a graphite color; it's a brown-based black and has the deepest body and most life of any supersaturated color I know of. And whites. I just painted all my doors—all 11.5 feet high—three shades of white: linen, bone, and off-white from the Benjamin Moore Cameo collection. It adds more dimension to the woodwork—depth and detail that is lacking in stingy twentieth-century construction."

**ERIC COHLER,**

**AN INTERIOR DESIGNER IN NEW YORK:**

"In fabrics I tend to favor neutrals and earth tones; for contrast I play with texture and fabric weight rather than color. I am also addicted to art and sculpture and take many fabric cues from a client's collection. The richer the collection of art, the simpler the background."

**CELESTE COOPER, AN INTERIOR DESIGNER
IN NEW YORK AND BOSTON:**

"I often use strong color in a foyer or a powder room, rooms one does not spend a lot of time in, rooms that one moves through and does not linger. I use it for drama, for the sense of the unexpected (the accepted theory is to paint small rooms light colors to make them seem bigger, which is a fallacy), and for how it fools the eye... when you walk into a neutral room after passing through a foyer painted a deep color the room appears even larger."

**LINDA CHASE,
AN INTERIOR DESIGNER IN CONNECTICUT:**

"I love color, especially the jewel tones. I've done projects with creams and off-whites, but my personal opinion is I don't think anything can impact space as quickly and with more impact than color, and I don't think there's anything that has more psychological impact on space than color."

**PARIS DESIGNER
SYLVIE NEGRE:**

"In the south of France, Corsica, for example, along the Mediterranean Sea where the sun is very bright, I will often choose very simple, light colors. A shade of beige on the floor, white or sand color on the walls, and doors in oak..."

**Sometimes the simplest palette makes for the most elegant. Here a milky-white room gets punched up with midnight black and gold via a pillow, lamp, and lacquer box. This is a great color combo for small and large spaces, and is both classy and classic.**

The all-natural textures of wood, glass, silver, and even seashells warm up a casual all-white room. Remember, white gives you a unique decorating freedom, a canvas of sorts, where collections of old and new objects and oddities can stand on the same plane.

White and gold in this bedroom provide a clean, crisp environment to show off the interesting shape of this room, architectural details, and the beautiful warmth of the hardwood floor. If you have interesting architectural details in your home, think about painting them with gold.

The focal points in this dining room are the scroll-backed, neutral-striped chairs all hugging the rich woodsy table. Your eye floats to the back of the room to the view, with no bright color to disrupt your trip. When you're designing your rooms, think about the view you want to create.

**RON FLEEGER, OF FLEEGER INC., NEW YORK, PRESIDENT AND CREATIVE DIRECTOR, INTERIOR DESIGN, ARCHITECTURAL DESIGN, HOME FURNISHINGS DESIGN:**

"I love neutrals. Neutrals doesn't mean boring. They provide a great place for people—inviting and cozy without knocking the hell out of them. Neutrals don't overpower people's personalities. When I think of space I think of people in there."

**MICHAEL SCANLON, AN INTERIOR DESIGNER IN BOSTON:**

"The most aggressive color we have is dead white. It jumps right out in your face because the walls reflect every bit of light that hits them."

**HALIMA TAHA, AMERICAN AND AFRICAN ART EXPERT, AND AUTHOR:**

"I love white walls because the absence of color allows me to experience the color that's here in the artwork. I allow white to create distance between art and the room, so the art seems to be hanging out..."

**RHODE ISLAND ARCHITECT**

**DAVID ANDREOZZI:**

"Color, like finish landscaping, is the one of the most ignored design elements in architecture today. Most architectural schools dismiss color as being secondary to the design... when in fact... most of the great architecture that provides the datum from which we as architects learn, use color and materials as in integral part of the design. When did this division in occur? It is tragic."

**BOSTON-BASED INTERIOR DESIGNER**

**MICHAEL SCANLON:**

"My approach to color comes from my experience as a painter. You discover when you're constructing on canvas that colors define distance. There's a technical term called aerial perspective, which deals with the way colors recede or come forward so when I approach applying color, the question is where do I want to place objects in space. I have a concept of the color wheel that is three dimensional. If you train yourself to think this way, you will be surprised by what you discover."

Another pleasant aspect of neutrals is that they stand quietly in the background, allowing the palette and textures of fabric and furnishings to shine through. The key is choosing the right neutral to let the best attributes of what you have take the spotlight. This is a perfect example; your eye takes in everything from the painting to the chair.

Cinnamon and toasted-brown partner well
in this elegant living room. It is far from
gloomy; in fact it seems to wrap you in
a lush warmth. If this is too much for
you to imagine in your home, consider
a modified version in smaller space
like a study or parlor.

A muted green wall works perfectly to create a clubby-feeling dining room, and allows bright artwork to serve as a welcome beacon.

"Everyone is drawn to different colors. Beige and creams are compromised colors. Continuing to use these means we're lacking expressiveness and joy by becoming the Wonder Bread colors. We're missing self-expression and just plain fun to always go there."

**This unusual wall covering with a hint of green gives this bedroom a quiet feeling, and works well to show off the warm and cool palette in the paintings. It also serves as a successful background color for the cluster of pen-and-ink drawings hung in gold and silver frames.**

**NEW YORK–BASED INTERIOR DESIGNER
ALEXANDRA STODDARD**

"To inspire yourself about using color, look at a garden, the sky, or a field."

**NEW YORK–BASED INTERIOR DESIGNER
MARRIO BUATTA**

"I hate white rooms… It makes me ill to be in them, and reminds me of a hospital."

**MINNESOTA-BASED ARCHITECT
KATHERINE HELLBRAND**

"I can't disassociate color and texture and composition. So for me, when I isolate color, I can't answer someone or what's best without seeing shapes, shadows, textures, and figures in space. It's very holistic. We may fiddle with one element but it's not possible."

**White takes the lead in this pretty dining area, allowing the warm color accents to define the space and the art. Those flaming heads just wouldn't have the same effect if the wall behind were bright yellow.**

**Cream, white, and gold ground this all-white room where artwork reigns supreme. With stunning views to the outdoor trees, the touches of wood inside—from the wood chairs to the carvings mantel-side—make the point that art and nature are joined.**

If you have a decidedly dramatic room, consider what you want to emphasize. Is it the furnishings, architecture, or views? The monochromatic palette makes this two-leveled space look relaxed, elegant, and serene.

# setting the mood

A simple black and white color scheme,
complete with stainless steel accents,
is the perfect way to emphasize a
breathtaking urban view.

It is almost second nature for most of us to relate mood and color. We have been trained our entire lives to see the connection—from the time we picked up our first toy fire engine, red said something to us. And so did the pinks and yellows that dressed little girls' dolls. This fashion partnership continues to surface in fashion statements as much as they do in our homes, offices, stores, and even our cars.

Who would argue that black is inappropriate to wear to a formal dinner party, or that a red velvet dress at Christmas is not right? We keep our high-rise offices gray and stiff to keep the mood business-like, and don gray suits to match. And imagine, if you can, how incongruous a pink Mercedes would be!

When it comes to our homes, color matches and combinations are critical to setting the mood and creating a very specific atmosphere. Colors, whether they're in your fabrics, rugs, wall coverings or window treatments all have the power to contribute to a room's mood.

Look through this chapter to see the way color combinations work for you, and with you. And realize that you can set your own stage for drama, romance, and energy by choosing the right mix.

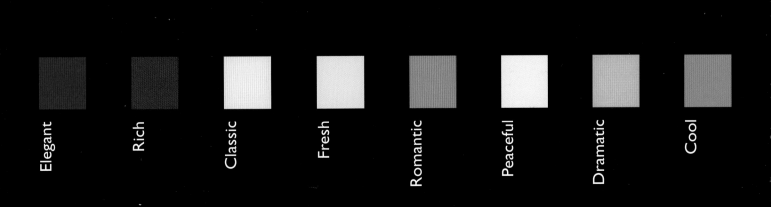

Elegant     Rich     Classic     Fresh     Romantic     Peaceful     Dramatic     Cool

Simple, two-color palettes easily create an elegant mood in a room, as demonstrated by the effective combination of rich cranberry and yellow accents in this bedroom. Imagine how beautiful this room looks when the trees outside the window have turned gold and red with fall, or are topped by creamy snow peaks. Consider how big a role views play in rooms before settling on a palette. You can complement the seasons or match them.

Perhaps you've been to the Orient, or Tuscany, and you would like to recreate the feeling you had there. It's easy to do so by introducing the right palette, and accent pieces of those places in your own home.

If you're designing a room from scratch think about carrying a color and graphic theme throughout. And don't forget how a bit of whimsy and playfulness can cheer you year round. Here, yellow is the star of the day.

**RON FLEEGER, OF FLEEGER INC., NEW YORK, PRESIDENT AND CREATIVE DIRECTOR, INTERIOR DESIGN, ARCHITECTURAL DESIGN, HOME FURNISHINGS DESIGN:**

"I think color can affect mood tremendously. If you use blue and white, people think of the sky and water, and it's relaxing. Gray, on the other hand, can suck you of all your energy... Red makes you feel exciting and hot, green makes you think of opulence and the outdoors. Color represents all those things of the life force, and produces different emotions."

**KAKI HOCKERSMITH, DESIGNER FOR THE WHITE HOUSE UNDER THE CLINTON ADMINISTRATION:**

"I relate color to nature. If you just look outside, nobody is inspired by a gray and dreary day, no flowers in the pots! If you think about why we love the spring and summer, it's because of the flowers, blue sky, and green grass. And if you are comfortable with that, why wouldn't you want that variety and cheerful color palette in your home? You can have those colors you love inside when it's cold and dreary outside!"

**NEW YORK INTERIOR DESIGNER
ALEXANDRA STODDARD:**

"Colors can make you smile. They give you a sense of wonder and hope. They heal, bring joy, and they are there for you like a warm puppy. I'm really concerned that if people can't express themselves with color, how can they express themselves? Why is it we are not able to have that joy—especially with so much sadness in the world?"

**CHRIS CASSON MADDEN: DESIGNER, AUTHOR, AND HGTV HOST**

"I'm often accused by people of being that lady who always talks about the punch of color! I love to point out the snap or punch of color though because color does bring a room to life. I'm sitting here right now in my little study and I have an old gilt mirror with a band of velvet, red ribbon around my Shaker boxes, and my raspberry red plaid chaise nearby... Diana Vreeland would be happy and proud to see me!"

**NEW YORK BASED INTERIOR DESIGNER ERIC COHLER:**

"Color, for me, sets the mood of my rooms and gives a heightened sense of scale and drama. I find that darker colors make walls recede and actually seem larger—rather than the reverse. Above all I like harmony in my colors."

When you're choosing wall colors and fabrics, you need to balance your love of a hue with the mood you're trying to achieve. Here, a dramatic and elegant space is also quiet and soothing with the mint green walls and peach fabric.

Choose your favorite color and bathe a
room in versions of it. Yellow, gold, and
touches of burnt orange with period furnishings create an Old World elegance in
this dining area.

When your ceiling looks like the facets of a highly polished diamond, there's really no need to detract with lots of objects d'art. This all-white bed floats like a giant cloud in this sensual sleep space.

This designer created a dining area that is relaxing and engaging. There's lots of texture and a variety of shapes that soothe and capture your eye. The minimal amount of color works well, giving the spotlight to art.

Deep brown walls might not come to mind for a bedroom, but look how it emphasizes design details and art in this room. The choice of a rich, red fabric flowing onto the wood floor sets the mood as quiet elegance.

**MARIO BUATTA,**

**INTERIOR DESIGNER, NEW YORK:**

"You need to have color in your life. It's what makes a dreary apartment happy. For most people though, they've fallen into the white thing, and it's boring! After my clients get over their fear of color, they're happy with the color in their apartments—especially after coming home from a gray city. Color affects your life."

**NEW YORK–BASED AUTHOR, LECTURER, BENJAMIN MOORE ARCHIVE CONSULTANT BARBARA MAYER:**

"I think most people do have an idea of how they want to decorate their room; often they want to emphasize a period—French, Modern, English, Arts and Crafts, and there are certain color choices that were accurate and used in many of these styles. If you want to create a Victorian room, you would be looking at upholstery in deep, rich colors, and walls in deep gold, as well as ruby reds, deep green, and a brilliant deep blue... By the same token, if you love neoclassical, it would be unlikely that you would use those colors. You would be using light, clear colors, like Wedgwood blue, pale green, and white. And there are combinations that can help you create the style you want. If you love the form of neoclassical furnishings, and you don't love the colors that reflect the style, there is nothing wrong with choosing the furniture form and a color scheme you like."

White on white, except for the ebony floor, creates a rather heavenly space and makes for the ultimate serene room. Color seeps in from the views, coloring the walls in different hues as the sun moves across the sky.

**You can bring the tropical island mood
inside, and hold that relaxed feeling by
simply mimicking the palette in your view!**

It's easy to keep the mood formal
and romantic with clean white walls
and period furnishings covered in rich,
subtly colored fabrics.

This city condo's calming color scheme—
a medley of neutrals—works well to
show off an art theme of faces.

**ZINA GLAZEBROOK,**
**INTERIOR DESIGNER, NEW YORK:**

"Find out what drives you in the room. Is it the fabric, a rug, a piece of glass? Take a look and jump off—take something alarming away from that object."

**CELESTE COOPER, INTERIOR DESIGNER,**
**NEW YORK AND BOSTON:**

"Sometimes one WANTS to camouflage... flaws in proportions, totally undistinguished architecture, problems in scale. Color can then work to take your mind's eye away from features you don't want to see. And something small in a color will balance something large and neutral."

Here is a bedroom that lifts the spirit. Planted like an indoor flower garden, a pane of glass is the only divider from the natural gardens' smell outside. No matter what the season, you can feel spring and summer's glory.

What else can you say about this room?
It's a natural palette that makes you
smile and feel warm and welcome. It
could work anywhere in your home.

**Deep purples and blues with random gold accents, provided for the most part through lighting fixtures, makes this space seem cavernous yet cozy.**

The surprise of lavender on the ceiling punctuates an open, airy bedroom. This technigue works well for rooms with little trim or molding and a modern sensibility.

**directory of designers**

## Featured Architects

**David Andreozzi**
**Andreozzi Architects**
232 Waseca Avenue
Barrington, RI 2806
Tel. 401-245-6800

**Bromley Caldari**
**Architects, Inc.**
242 West 27th Street
New York, NY 10001
Tel. 212-620-4250

**Arthur Collin**
1a Berry Place
London ECIV OJD
England
Tel. 0171-490-3520

**F2 Inc.**
**Faulding Architecture**
11 East 22nd Street
New York, NY 10010
Tel. 212-253-1513

**Lindsay Associates**
332 Newbury Street
Boston, MA 02115
617-536-5054
& 461 2nd Street, Suite 120
San Francisco, CA 94107
Tel. 415-957-1103

**Nik Randall**
**Brooks Stacey Randall**
**Architects & Technology**
**Consultants**
New Hibernia House
Winchester Walk
London SE19AG
England
Tel. 0171-403-0707

**SALA Inc.**
**(Architect Katherine**
**Hillbrand)**
43 Main Street, Suite 410
Minneapolis, MN 55414
Tel. 612-379-3037

## Featured Designers and Color and Home Furnishings Experts

**Antine Associates Inc.**
15 Industrial Ave.
Fairview, NJ 07022
Tel. 201-941-8048

**Jeffrey Bilhuber**
330 East 59th Street
New York, NY 10022
Tel. 212-308-9888

**Lee Bogart Interior Design**
250 Birch Hill Road
Locust Valley, NY 11560
Tel. 516-676-3881

**Laura Bohn Design**
**Associates**
30 West 26th Street
New York, NY 10010
Tel. 212-645-3636

**Mario Buatta**
120 East 80th Street
New York, NY 10021
Tel. 212-988-6811

**Linda Chase Associates, Inc.**
482 Town Street
East Haddam, CT 06423
Tel. 860-873-9499

**Christopher Coleman Design**
70 Washington Street
Brooklyn, NY 11201
Tel. 718-222-8984

**Celeste Cooper**
1415 Boylston Street
Boston, MA 02116
Tel. 617-826-5667

**Eric Cohler Inc.**
872 Madison Avenue
New York, NY 10021
Tel. 212-737-8600

Treena Crochet
**A Matter of Style, Ltd.**
304 Newbury Street
Boston, MA 02115
Tel. 617-943-4253
Crochet@styleltd.com

**D'Aquino Monaco Inc.**
180 Varicle Street, 4th Floor
New York, NY 10012
Tel. 212-929-9787

**Duffy Design Group**
516 East 2nd Street
South Boston, MA 02127
Tel. 617-464-4640

**Eva Dewitz**
65 East India Row
Boston, MA 02110
Tel. 617-742-5221

**Drysdale Design
Associates Inc.**
78 Kalorama Circle, NW
Washington, D.C. 20009
Tel. 202-588-0700

**Ron Fleeger Design**
131 East 23rd Street
New York, NY 10010
Tel. 212-477-5729
ron@fleeger.com

**Clare Fraser
Fraser Associates**
133 East 64th Street
New York, NY 10022
Tel. 212-737-3479

**Kaki Hockersmith**
5116 Kavanaugh Blvd.
Little Rock, AK 72207
Tel. 501-666-6966
kaki@aristotle.net

**William Hodgins**
232 Clarendon Street
Boston, MA 02116
Tel. 617-262-9538

**Kelly Hoppen**
**2 Alma Studios**
32 Stratford Road
London WB 6QF
England
Tel. 0171-938-4151
Aposter@kellyhoppen.co.uk

**Thomas Jayne Studio, Inc.**
136 East 57th Street
New York, NY 02116
Tel. 212-838-9080

**Alexander Julian**
P.O. Box 308
Budd Lake, NJ 07828
Tel. 1-800-776-7986, ext 101

**Michelle Lamb
Marketing Directions, Inc.**
7205 Ohms Lane, Suite 175
Minneapolis, MN 55439
Tel. 952-893-1245
info@trendcurve.com

**Chris Madden Inc.**
88 Purchase Street
Rye, NY 10580
Tel. 914-921-2847
www.chrismadden.com

**Barbara Mayer**
53 Crosspond Road
Pound Ridge, NY 10576
Tel. 914-763-3467
barbm3882@aol.com

**Susan Moore**
1514 West 25th Street
Minneapolis, MN 55405
Tel. 612-377-3386
smoore5100@aol.com

**Claire Murray**
Tel. 800-252-4733
www.clairemurray.com

**Sylvie Negre**
Violaine D'Harambure
37 Rue Raynouard
Paris 75016
France

**Jennifer Post**
25 East 67th Street
New York, NY 10021
Tel. 212-734-7994

**James Rixner, Inc.**
121 Morton Street
New York, NY 10014
Tel. 212-206-7439

**HGTV's Joe Ruggerio**
www.ruggerioideas.com

**Michael J. Scanlon**
1 Design Center Place
Boston, MA 02210
Tel. 617-439-4500

**Eric Schmitt**
10 Rue de Nemours
Villers sous Grez
Paris 77760
France

**Charles Spada Interiors**
1 Design Center Place
Boston, MA 02210
Tel. 617-951-0008

**Alexandra Stoddard Inc.**
1125 Park Avenue
New York, NY 10128
Tel. 212-427-6434

**Karen Sugarman**
29 Newbury Street
Boston, MA 02116
Tel. 617-424-6688

**Sarah Susanka
Author,** *The Not So Big House &
Creating the Not So Big House*
www.notsobig.com

**Tina Sutton Fashion
Services Inc.**
11 Linden Place
Brookline, MA 02445
Tel. 617-232-6114

**Halima Taha
150 Ascan Avenue**
Forest Hills, NY 11375
Tel. 718-268-2895
Htaha@aol.com

**Jean Townsend/Droll Design**
50 Grove Street
Salem, MA 01970
Tel. 978-741-3231
www.drolldesigns.com

**ZG Design**
10 Wireless Road
East Hampton, NY 11937
Tel. 631-329-7486

**directory of photographers**

CJ Walker/Charles Spada Interiors, 35; 64; 66; 67; 70;

71 (bottom); 75 (top); 76 (top); 90; 91 (bottom); 101; 102; 112

(bottom); 114; 115 (bottom); 119

Stan Schnier/Jennifer Post Design, 37; 84; 92; 93

©Philip Ennis/Christopher Coleman Interior Design, 40; 44

©Sargent/Charles Spada Interiors, 45 (top); 112 (top); 113

Tim Street-Porter 103 (right); 111 (bottom)

Tim Street-Porter/Beateworks, 51; 57 (top)

Andrew Lautman/Drysdale, Inc., 56

Tim Lee/Anthony Antine, Antine Shin, LLC, 62; 75 (bottom); 97;

Elizabeth Glasgow/Zina Glazebrook, ZG Design, 63 (left); 68; 69;

73; 78; 81; 86; 87 (both); 110; 116; 117

Marisa Pellegrini/Anthony Antine, Antine Shin, LLC,

72 (top); 95 (top);

Marisa Pelligrini/Ho Sang Shin, Antine Shin, LLC, 100 (bottom)

Durston Saylor/Anthony Antine, Antine Shin, LLC,

74; 106; 107 (top)

Tom McCavera/James Rixner, Inc., 79

Peter Paige/Anthony Antine, Antine Shin, LLC, 94; 95 (bottom)

Richard Barnes/Bromley/Caldari Architects 103 left, 104

Peter Margonelli/Linda Chase Associates, Inc., 108

Glenn Daidone, Boston/Dennis Duffy Design 111 (top); 115 (top)

Jaime Ardiles-Arce/Bromley-Caldari Architects, 11

the new home color book

# acknowledgments

Thank you to Shawna Mullen, my editor, and all the designers, architects, and color experts for sharing your projects, words of wisdom, and humor. You gave this book its bones.

And finally, special thanks to Libbie Johnson for introducing me to so many talented people.

the new home color book

# dedication

This book is dedicated to my late mother, Katie, whose flower gardens, house, and wardrobe were all about her passion for color.

# about the author

Anna Kasabian has written on numerous topics including living, gardening, dining, traveling, and antiquing in New England, but her great passion is exploring modern interiors and architecturally significant homes, hotels, inns, and gardens. She is the author of *Designing Interiors with Tile: Creative Ideas with Ceramics, Stone, and Mosaic; East Coast Rooms;* and *Kids' Rooms* (all by Rockport Publishers). As a contributor to *Cooking Spaces*, she explored the at-home kitchens of some of the most respected chefs and food writers in the United States and abroad. Kasabian's byline regularly appears in *The Boston Globe, Boston Magazine, New England Travel & Life,* and *Woman's Day.* She also scouts for HGTV, and has appeared on the popular network. She has been featured on National Public Radio's Boston affiliate, WBUR.